It's a
MIRACLE!

It's Green Miracle...
&
It Saved My Life!

Dee Simmons

It's a Miracle! It's Green Miracle..

It's a Miracle! It's Green Miracle ...& It Saved My Life!
Published by Dee Simmons

This book or part thereof may not be reproduced in any form, stored in a retrieval system or transmitted in any form by any means - electronic, mechanical, photocopy, recording or otherwise - without prior written permission of the authors, except as provided by Untied States of America copyright law.

This book is not intended to provide medical advice or to take the place of medical advice and treatment from your personal physician. Readers are advised to consult their own doctors or other qualified health professionals regarding the treatment of their medical problems. Neither the publisher nor the author takes any responsibility for any possible consequences from any treatment, action or application of medicine, supplement, herb or preparation to any person reading or following the information in this book. If readers are taking prescription medications, again, they should consult with their physicians and not take themselves off of medicines to start supplementation or nutrition program without the proper supervision of a physician.

Printed in the United States of America

Table of Contents

Introduction

We all desire to live long, healthy lives. However, chemicals, the environment, our diet, and stress take a toll on our health and wellness.

The purpose of this book is to give you proven nutrition information so you may achieve great health benefits. It's all about prevention and taking charge of your life by treating the cause of illness rather than the symptoms.

Twenty years ago, I learned how important it is to take charge of my health and wellness when I was faced with a life-threatening disease. The healing miracle of green foods played and continues to play a vital role in both my recovery and my total remission from breast cancer. I am so pleased to be able to share my findings and experiences in the hopes that you will be spared illness and that you will, instead, attain optimum wellness.

Since my bout with cancer, my days now are precious. In the past I always took them for granted. Make each day count. Live life to its fullest, thank God for your health, and...be grateful for every day He gives you!

Blessings and Good Health,

Dee Simmons

Chapter One

My Story…
Searching for a Miracle

Before cancer, as a highly successful businesswoman with widely publicized and lucrative fashion showrooms in New York and Dallas, I believed I was living the best possible life. At forty-seven I was a former beauty queen, a beloved wife, mother of a gorgeous and talented daughter, blessed with high energy, and – I thought – excellent health.

Then came the diagnosis of breast cancer, a modified radical mastectomy, and reconstructive surgery. I was blessed to have the finest medical treatment and a successful outcome. But the nagging question remained: Why did I get cancer? There was no history of cancer in my family, I wasn't overweight, and I didn't fit into the high-risk criteria for breast cancer. All of my life I had been thin, and like so many, I associated being thin with being healthy. This is a false concept and a very dangerous point of view.

I now believe one major factor in me having breast cancer was my poor eating habits. As a child, my mother was very strict about eating healthy and avoiding those foods that were not nutritious. When I was old enough to make my own eating choices, I took the opposite road. By today's standard I would be classified as a sugar addict. You won't believe what I could eat.

My day began with a half-dozen chocolate chip cookies and two cups of coffee before even saying hello to anyone. Then I ate a big breakfast. At lunch I might eat a pint of ice cream or drink a malt. I baked every day. If I made a pie, my husband and my daughter might have one small slice each. I would eat the rest of it by myself before the day was over.

So many times we fail ourselves in the good health department and try to justify our diets by saying, "There's nothing wrong with eating a few cookies, or even eating a whole pie." Because we have a small waistline or we may even work out, we think it's okay to splurge.

This is the trap so many fall into, and before long the toll of a poor diet results in a very loud wake-up call...cancer or some other form of degenerative disease.

I can't imagine eating a whole pie now, but I think you get the picture of my past bad eating habits. Big changes and a radical new approach to my health and wellness was on the horizon.

Thus began my quest to search out the best in health and nutrition.

Knowledge is powerful and can be our greatest weapon in the fight for health and wellness.

When I was diagnosed with cancer, I went in search of every bit of information I could find. Believing that "knowledge is power," I knew that I needed all the facts to empower me to tackle breast cancer head-on.

As I recuperated, a paper with an amazing story came into my hands. I read a cancer survivor's testimony about her cure through nutritional supplementation and was intrigued. Knowing almost nothing about nutrition, which at that time was largely ignored by the medical community, I immediately charged into a leading local health food store and began learning about vitamins, free radicals, the immune system, and a host of other topics which I knew virtually nothing about. I soon discovered the importance of green foods and their immune-boosting properties. This was the first alternative product I tried on my road to discovering optimum health.

Soon I became a convert, telling my cancer story to everyone and sharing my ever-growing knowledge about nutrition. Doctors, not trained in medical school about the subject of nutrition, began referring patients to me for counseling they were unable to provide.

Many long days and countless late night telephone calls were spent encouraging and informing cancer patients who rang from every part of the globe.

Conventional and complimentary medicines should not be at odds with each other, rather each enhances the other. I believe intelligent people should seek a balance, accepting the best of science and the best of nature.

Five years after my bout with cancer, tragedy struck my life again. I lost my best friend, my mother, to cancer. When Mother died from cancer, we declared all-out war against the disease. My husband Glenn and I often speak of the amazing turn in the road my destiny took, and how radically our lives and personal commitments have changed as a result. One of the good things a cancer experience accomplishes is to deepen our compassion for others needs and desires. In my own family, many things changed after I had cancer. Relationships became a priority as never before.

Cancer often makes people angry or bitter. Like any other cancer patient, I hate cancer and I know how it feels to be told that you have a life threatening disease. I also know how it feels to hear that your special loved one has cancer. Cancer took the life of my mother in just four short weeks. Years later, my only sister was diagnosed with breast cancer. With earlier detection, modern scientific treatments, and a good nutritional regimen, my sister is now a thriving survivor. But the story does not stop there. In June of 2001, my father lost his battle with prostate cancer.

Cancer is no respecter of persons. Today this dreaded disease strikes any age, gender, race or social status. The good news, according to the American Cancer Society, is that this year millions will survive and recover from cancers of every type.

Cancer or any degenerative disease is a challenge, but don't underestimate your own ability to rise to the challenge. We all have far more inner resources than we realize. Standing tall and taking charge of our health and wellness generates a sense of control, which enables us to realize we are not victims, but survivors!

My mother's death inspired me to learn more about the causes of cancer and nutrition. I became an avid student of the scientific advancements which were taking place in the field of nutrition by traveling extensively to learn from some of the leading scientists, doctors, and nutritionists in the world. I became aware of a problem during my travels. Most nutritional companies with good products typically had several very good products, while other products in the line would be inferior. No product line was consistently providing superior products in every category.

In regards to nutritional products, I believe

 Cost should never prohibit the use of top-quality ingredients.

 Each item in a product line should meet highest quality standards

 Cleanliness and pharmaceutical-level laboratory standards are essential.

Having tried most every nutrition product on the market, I was dissatisfied with the quality and effectiveness of most brands. I dreamed of creating a complete line of high-quality, all-natural nutritional formulas that would meet MY standards. Today, that dream is a reality!

Ten years following my cancer experience, I established a business which distributes nutritional and skin care products. I had initially created these products for my own use, insisting that the formulations result in a pure, high-quality, and effective product. Glenn suggested that I name my company *"Ultimate Living,"* because we were determined to aim for the highest and best living, not just the marginal health so many of us are content to accept.

Ultimate Living unveiled its first phase of nutritional products on July 1, 1996. We now have over 33 pharmaceutical grade nutritional products in the line, and a total of 23 skincare and cosmetic products.

Ultimate Living continues to research and create, in my opinion, the most potent line of nutritional and wellness aids available anywhere. I insist on that. You might say I'm betting my life, at least to a significant degree, on it. It is with true confidence that we offer our line of immune enhancing items to cancer patients, survivors, and others who know the vital importance of supporting their physical systems with the best in nutrition.

Cancer patients and others always ask me, "What did you do?" First, let me stress, *I do not prescribe*, but I can share my story and offer information on how I took charge of my health. I had to change my diet, and by that I mean a complete lifestyle change. I had to become as healthy as I possibly could. I could no longer drift along, neglecting proper nutrition and exercising a few days or weeks at a time.

It isn't enough to look good; we must also be healthy if we are to experience *Ultimate Living*.

Through my years of counseling cancer patients, I have never known anyone to beat the disease that did not change their dietary habits to include more fruits and vegetables...ever! One does not need to wait for a cancer diagnosis to make this dietary change.

The American Cancer Society says that we can stave off many cancers by increasing our intake of fresh fruits and vegetables...particularly dark, leafy greens. With five or more daily-recommended servings, in this world of fast food and take-out, most of us find it difficult, if not impossible, to meet the required amounts of fruits and vegetables we need to simply "keep up."

While we all know that there is no substitute for fresh, organic produce, the reality is that very few of us have the time to prepare the optimum diet for our bodies. *Ultimate Living's* **Green Miracle** bridges that nutritional gap, and is an incredibly easy and effective way to supplement your diet with the fruits and vegetables needed to boost the entire immune system.

Chapter Two

Boosting Your Immune System

Like many other people today, I've become aware of the importance of doing everything I can to enhance my body's immune system. Admittedly, it took my cancer diagnosis to teach me to stay mindful of my natural defense system and truly respect this built-in life preserver.

Actually, it took very little study of the subject to convince me of two powerful truths:

1. Cancer, like so many other serious illnesses, results from a lowered immune system.

2. We are, as the Bible tells us, *fearfully and wonderfully made* – from brain to toes, each individual cell in the human body is a complex structure with components numbering in the thousands. The Immune System is comprised of white blood cells specialized to provide the body with resistance to disease. When harmful microorganisms (e.g. bacteria, viruses, fungi), cancer cells, or toxic molecules enter the body, it is the immune system that is charged with recognizing these invaders and destroying them.

Is it possible to produce healthier cells and strengthen our immune system's functions? And if so, how do we go about it? Twenty years ago, one of my friends asked her allergist, a noted specialist, those same questions. "There's nothing you can do," he told the middle-aged asthma patient. "The immune system wanes as the body ages; and yours is aging."

That statement, widely believed at the time, no longer is accepted as fact. It is true that one's immunity against bacteria, viruses, and chronic diseases may lessen over the years due to poor diet, tobacco use, lack of sufficient sleep, excess physical and emotional stress, and a host of environmental causes. Cancer, for example, is a long-term process; cell damage often takes place over decades before a tumor results.

Today, a growing body of medical research provides overwhelming evidence that there is much we can do to avert the downhill slide of our immune system. During the past decade especially, many cancer survivors like myself have made it our business to learn what the immune system is, what it does, and how we can strengthen it.

In the name of building a better immune system and fighting off cancer, some of us do some pretty extreme things – usually, of course, without our doctors' sanctions. I did a lot of experimentation, trying this or that potential remedy I'd hear about, and my doctor would warn me, "Just don't harm yourself, Dee, or spend a lot of money on pure quackery."

But that was before physicians and the lay public knew much about the effects of nutrition, food supplements, and much else that is common knowledge today. In those days, I mostly went out on my own, contacting some of the world's leading research physicians I had heard about, flying to other cities to interview them and obtain their recommendations. Much that I learned then in my own relentless searching is common knowledge that is easily attainable today.

It is essential that we understand which dietary or nutritional supplements work at the cellular level to offer help early, before degenerative or chronic diseases get a head start. Superb immune system enhancers, in many cases, actually reduce early tumors or heal lesions.

There is little doubt these days that nutraceuticals can play a powerful role in preventing and even reversing disease. Many scientific studies during the past decade alone, have reported strong and convincing evidence to support the use of well-chosen nutritional supplements. Obviously, years of study have erased any doubts I may have had about their value.

However, I urge everyone to research the subject thoroughly before entering into a supplementation plan. Since each person's life, health history, metabolism, and disease characteristics are unique, we need to follow certain prudent guidelines.

 Discuss your needs with a health care practitioner.

Beware of misinformation and false claims.

 Consider carefully the quality of the supplements and the quality of the science that supports them. **All supplements are not created equal.**

The billions Americans invest in dietary supplements alone show how serious we are about boosting our immune system, achieving better health, and living disease-free lives.

Ultimate Living is dedicated to building a healthier world by providing the most effective supplements to restore and maintain vibrant health.

Green Miracle is the flagship product of my nutrition company, *Ultimate Living*. It is a pure and powerful collection of nutrients and phytochemicals important for optimal health and vitality. Three scoops of **Green Miracle** provide the daily-recommended servings of fruits and vegetables, plus it is live food for live people!

Chapter Three

What's So Miraculous About Green Foods?

In today's world, "eating right" is becoming more and more of a challenge. Given the over-processing of foods and current depletive farming practices, we are deprived of many of the vitamins, minerals, and nutrients our body needs for a well functioning immune system and the energy to get us through the day.

The U.S. Surgeon General attributes two thirds of all deaths in the United States to poor diet! According to the American Institute for Cancer Research (AICR), we need five or more servings a day of green leafy vegetables and fruits. Unfortunately, ninety-five percent of Americans never achieve this.

In fact, the U.S. Department of Agriculture states that on any given day, fifty percent of the population eat no vegetables, seventy percent eat no vegetables or fruits rich in vitamin C, and eighty percent eat no vegetables or fruits rich in carotenoids. The shocking news stated by the U.S. Department of Agriculture is that less than ten percent of the population consumes three servings of fruits or vegetables per day. Is it any wonder that disease and illness are so prevalent?

Green vegetables contain twenty times more essential nutrients than other foods. If we fail to eat green leafy vegetables on a daily basis, valuable cleansing, building and eliminative functions fail to work properly. This contributes to a broken down (compromised) immune system that can lead to degenerative disease.

Green foods offer marvelous nutritional and health benefits. They are rich in vitamins, minerals, fiber, calcium, natural enzymes, protein, essential amino acids and many other nutrients needed to cleanse, balance, detoxify and regenerate our bodies.

Green foods may be the most effective natural cure for osteoporosis, arthritis, diabetes, low energy, digestive disorders and many other degenerative diseases. So how do green foods work?

While green foods contain an abundant list of vitamins, minerals, proteins, enzymes, chlorophyll and more, green foods are actually catalysts that support chemical chain reactions within your body.

Most disease starts when incomplete chemical and metabolic reactions occur during digestion, respiration, and elimination, which creates acidic toxic waste in the body. This ultimately interferes with cellular replication.

As we know, each cell in the body is responsible for replicating itself. During cellular "reproduction" chromosomes split into chromatides and reassemble into genes. If they do not match up properly, cellular defects cause aging, bone loss, heart disease and even cancer. Green foods help *balance the body* and create an environment where disease is less likely to occur.

Green foods such as Green Kamut®, Wheat Grass, Barley Grass, Hawaiian Spirulina and Chlorella help the body neutralize and remove toxins. In addition, they are high in potassium, calcium and phytochemicals.

Many nutritional scientists and health experts believe the phytochemicals and phytonutrients found in green foods are essential for optimum health and the absorption of nutrients by the body, because they keep the body alkaline and thus able to more readily fight off disease.

Phytochemicals and phytonutrients are found naturally in all plant life, including fruits and vegetables. They give plants their medicinal qualities and allow them to ward off deterioration and toxic influences. These preventive and healing qualities are passed on to you when you consume any plant food.

The disease-fighting potential of phytochemicals is so promising, the National Cancer Institute launched a five-year, multimillion-dollar project to find, isolate and study these amazing substances.

Time magazine called phytochemicals "the new frontier in cancer-prevention research" and "the next big thing" in health science ("Beyond Vitamins," April, 1994). Many scientists are amazed at the effects phytochemicals have on our cells and, in many cases, the effects they have on malignant cells.

Some of the most amazing government funded studies have been largely ignored by the popular media. For example, one study has shown how adding green food to even the best diet can increase cancer prevention dramatically.

Studies at the Center for Disease Control show that people who eat a high fiber, low fat diet decreased their risk for colon/rectal cancer by less than ten percent, yet after adding five servings of greens to the same low fat, high fiber diet their risk fell by nearly forty percent!

Other studies show a lack of green vegetables increases breast cancer risk nearly twenty-five percent, with skin cancer results being very similar.

According to Harvard researchers, one of the most important things anyone can do to avoid cancer is to consume more dark green foods.

I'm convinced that green foods were an important factor in rebuilding my immune system when I had my bout with breast cancer. Twenty years later, I believe taking **Green Miracle** everyday is why I have so much energy and stamina. Plus, I don't have to worry about getting my nine servings of fruits and veggies. It's all in my **Green Miracle**.

The main reason I supplement my diet with ***Ultimate Living's*** **Green Miracle** is that food produced today is grown in soil that often lacks the nutrients our bodies need for building new, strong, healthy, and vital cells. The plants that become **Green Miracle** are grown in nutrient rich soil and contain phytonutrients needed for optimum health.

Consuming the proper amount of phytonutrients is very important to the quality of health an individual achieves and maintains. The health benefits from these valuable nutrients assist in fighting heart disease, arthritis, and cancer growths. It also improves vision, increases energy levels, improves skin health, and even diminishes the effects of the common cold and allergies.

Green foods contain more than 100 vitamins, minerals, fibers and other beneficial substances. Green foods are the *superstars of nutrition* because of the high content of phytochemicals and nutrients they contain.

One very important and power-packed nutrient found in all green foods is chlorophyll. Chlorophyll is what makes green foods green. This green pigment has many health-giving features including the ability to detoxify the body, fight free radicals, reduce inflammation, and assist in increased formation of oxygen-carrying red blood cells.

Chlorophyll is different from other nutrients due to its nearly identical chemical structure to human blood, which oxygenates and energizes the entire body. Scientific studies have shown malignant cells cannot thrive in the presence of oxygen. Therefore, by consuming the proper amount of green leafy vegetables on a daily basis, the risk of cancer may very well be decreased.

Chlorophyll also acts as a strong antioxidant to improve and build the immune system. *It is believed by many that there is only one true disease and that is a compromised immune system.* With today's hurried lifestyles, environmental hazards and everyday stress, the main focus for everyone should be to build and strengthen their immune system.

Low pH or over acidity in the system often is the root cause of many diseases. It begins when our blood is deprived of alkaline ash food that creates a low alkaline buffer reserve in our tissue. Alkaline ash foods are foods that when burned leave an alkaline residue, we also call these alkaline forming foods.

As the alkaline reserve is *used up* by our blood, minerals such as potassium, magnesium, and calcium are leached from bones and other tissues to buffer excess lactic, uric, and other damaging acids. Pulling minerals from bones and other tissues to *buffer* acid weakens their structure and results in bone loss, arthritis, and ultimately osteoporosis. This stresses normal metabolic function.

Another defensive measure is to store the ammonia acids in the kidneys in an attempt to conserve the alkaline buffer reserve. This ultimately leads to kidney stones, hormone imbalance, and contributes to the cellular stress that leads to disease.

The leading cause of low pH and over-acidity is the consumption of processed foods (carbohydrates, sugar, white flour, hydrogenated oils), meat, protein, and carbonated beverages. The best way to create a strong alkaline reserve is to consume alkaline–ash foods like green foods, which will in turn balance the pH of the body, allowing other important aspects of immune defense to be unleashed.

Green foods also are rich in hundreds of active, natural enzymes. When we are born, our body comes equipped with enough enzymes to last us for the rest of our lives. However, as a result of our lifestyles, diet and the environment, our body's enzyme reserve is constantly being depleted and we no longer have a sufficient amount of enzymes to last us a lifetime.

What is an enzyme? Enzymes are proteins that catalyze or accelerate chemical reactions. Almost all processes that take place in cells need enzymes in order to occur at significant rates. Digestive enzymes aid in proper digestion and fight off bacteria, carcinogens, and viruses. Enzymes also assist in bringing the body into perfect pH balance. If this balance is upset, cell metabolism suffers, which can lead to fatigue or serious health problems.

Don't be discouraged! There is a way to help keep your pH balanced! By eating a diet rich in green foods, depleted enzymes can be replenished aiding in proper absorption, digestion and elimination.

Green foods also supply our body with a rich source of vegetable proteins. These lightweight proteins enhance the immune system, increase reproductive functions, and serve as the building blocks for lean connective tissue. Strong connective tissues increase the strength of bone and muscular structure. This is very important for individuals with high risk of osteoporosis.

Diet plays an important role in how our body reacts, rebuilds, and resists illness and disease. The realization that foods can protect against and treat disease is not something new. In fact, it has been stated throughout the centuries, "It is diet that maintains true health and becomes the best medicine." Green foods, with an abundance of vitamins, minerals, enzymes and other essential nutrients are a quick and simple way to move towards optimum health.

The time has come for us to get back to the basics. The foundation to a healthy diet is eating a variety of foods including plenty of green foods, grains, nuts, fruits and vegetables. The occasional tossed salad or apple a day cannot really make a difference in a strong foundation for wellness.

The USDA conducted a study on the benefits of improved diets rich in fruits and vegetables. This study revealed several interesting health benefits such as: reduction of heart and vascular problems by twenty-five percent, reduction of the number of people with arthritis by fifty percent, and reduction of the number of deaths and acute conditions from cancer by twenty percent.

The saying "you are what you eat" could be restated as: "what you eat determines your healthy destiny!"

Today the green food revolution is here to stay, and not surprisingly, millions of people have taken notice both in the USA and worldwide. Armed with published studies, amazing testimonials, and public service announcements by government institutions to eat your fruits and vegetables, green food advocates are winning the hearts and minds of some of the most renowned doctors and oncologists in America who offer greens to cancer patients as part of an integrative therapy program.

It's time to unleash the power of green foods. Simple lifestyle changes can be the determining factor in your future health and wellness. Include fresh dark green leafy vegetables in your diet and good quality nutritional supplements.

Ultimate Living's **Green Miracle** is an amazing simple food which contains over eighty ingredients. Each ingredient is specifically chosen to enhance and complement the other, and most importantly to deliver their precious nutritional content directly to your cells.

Chapter Four

A Health Food Store in a Can

Ultimate Living's **Green Miracle** is truly a health food store in a can. Not only is taking **Green Miracle** one of the best things you can do for your health, but it is also convenient and economical.

Ultimate Living's **Green Miracle Powder and Capsules** are manufactured to USP Pharmacopia/Pharmaceutical standards. Each product batch includes a Certificate of Content verifying the product ingredients and the Director of Quality Assurance approves it. Also, the Food and Drug Administration (FDA) has access to all production charts, analysis charts, and records.

In selecting good quality nutritional supplements, it is important to look at all ingredients to make sure the formulation is pure without coloring, flavoring or preservatives. Manufacturing to USP pharmaceutical standards insures all raw materials are logged, tagged, and identified by a Ph.D. Chemist for content, purity, and lack of microbiological contamination.

Green Miracle is a superior formulation, which includes over eight thousand milligrams of organic and all-natural ingredients. **Green Miracle** ingredients are grown in nutrient rich soil, free of pesticides and harmful chemicals. This incredibly potent soil is utilized in the cultivation of selected seeds that have never been hybridized or crossbred, and have never been exposed to chemical cultivation.

Plants are grown and harvested specifically to preserve their miraculous protein, vitamins, enzymes, and mineral rich qualities. The plants are harvested and processed in a timely manner as well, preserving the maximum amount of nutritional value for our products. Because of the timeliness of processing the plants, *Ultimate Living's* **Green Miracle** contains very high pH level ingredients with higher chlorophyll, more enzymes, and more lightweight protein and trace minerals.

Ultimate Living's dehydration methods are truly state-of-the-art and do not require the use of corn-based starches such as Maltodextrin. **Green Miracle** is a <u>LIVE</u> food supplement, which contains no binders, no fillers, no artificial color and no preservatives of any kind.

The essential vitamins, minerals, nutrients, amino acids, chlorophyll, trace minerals, and enzymes found naturally in **Green Miracle** can enhance health and wellness. By consuming a proper balance of pure whole foods like **Green Miracle**, improved blood glucose control may be achieved.

In order to halt the rise of degenerative diseases like diabetes, hypoglycemia, and other blood sugar problems, we need to consume living foods.

Serving Size 3 scoops Servings Per Container 30	
Amount Per Serving	
Calories 30	Calories from Fat 10
Total Fat	1g
Saturated Fat	0g
Cholesterol	0mg
Sodium	15mg
Potassium	115mg
Total Carbohydrate	4g
Dietary Fiber	1g
Sugars	1g
Protein	2g

Many degenerative diseases are nutrition related. The human body is designed so that every cell, organ, vessel, muscle, tissue, bone and ligament work together as a network defense to fight illness. The success of this network defense depends upon the quality and proper balance of fuel it receives.

When we feed our bodies a high-quality diet low in sugars, fats and carbohydrates, the major risk factors for chronic diseases such as obesity, high blood pressure, high cholesterol, heart disease, diabetes, hypoglycemia, kidney disease and cancer are lowered.

Ultimate Living **Green Miracle** includes the proper balance of nutrients needed to fuel the vital areas of the body. Ingredients found in **Green Miracle** include:

Green Kamut® Powder
A non-hybrid strain of wheat that is generally regarded as the purest, and therefore least allergy-inducing wheat. An

exceptionally high-energy wheat rich in protein, minerals, magnesium, zinc, amino acids, lipids, lightweight protein, antioxidants, chlorophyll, essential fatty acids, trace minerals and probiotics. Green Kamut® helps to cleanse, detoxify, rebuild, and fortify at the cellular level while boosting the immune system. It increases energy levels, combats fatigue, and aids in maintaining the body's proper acid/alkaline balance.

Wheat Grass, Barley Grass & Oat Grass
100% natural and organic whole food grasses grown pesticide and herbicide free. An excellent source of antioxidants, phytonutrients, trace minerals, vitamins, beta carotene, chlorophyll, folic acid, vitamin C, B-complex, amino acids, fiber, enzymes and nucleic acids. These grasses are highly beneficial in alkalizing the body.

Hawaiian Spirulina
Spirulina Pacifica from Hawaii is grown without the use of pesticides or herbicides. Spirulina is a highly absorbable source of minerals, mixed carotenoids, phytonutrients, B-vitamins, GLA and essential amino acids. Spirulina Pacifica is the richest source of protein in the plant world – sixty percent protein – three times that of beef. In addition, it helps to neutralize acidity caused by an excess of meats, sugars, dairy, starches, stimulants and environmental toxins.

Chlorella
Contains the highest percentage of chlorophyll in the plant world, which promotes detoxification. Chlorella is rich in nucleic acids (RNA/DNA), which helps maintain cellular protection and raise energy levels. Chlorella is known as the "King of Alkaline Forming Foods," helping to maintain a good pH balance and

revitalize the whole body. Chlorella contains more beta-carotene and iron than spinach and more vitamin B-12 than beef liver.

Rice Bran

Derived from the bran and outside covering of the rice kernel. Source of gamma oryzanol (a phytosterol unique to rice), vitamin E and lecithin-like phytonutrients.

Flax Seed

Flax is considered to be one of the most pure, rich sources of essential fatty acids. It contains a high percentage of alpha linolenic acid (ALA). Flax is very high in lignans, which have anti-viral, anti-bacterial, and anti-tumor properties. Flax seed also contains a high level of Omega-3 oils. In addition, it provides a mucilogenous texture rich in fiber and beneficial to the intestinal tract.

Bee Pollen

A perfect food rich in B vitamins and antioxidants, including lycopene, selenium, beta-carotene, vitamin C, vitamin E and other flavonoids.

Royal Jelly

One of the richest natural sources of pantothenic acid (vit B-5), also known as the anti-stress vitamin. Royal jelly is rich in protein, vitamins, minerals, enzymes, and contains 22 different amino acids. It is renowned for its antibacterial properties.

Oat Bran

Outer husk area of oat grain – exceptionally rich in fiber; research findings indicate reduction in cholesterol following regular ingestion.

Apple Fiber
Contains both soluble and insoluble fiber and is wonderful for its ability to cleanse the intestines, bind to cholesterol, heavy metals, and carcinogens, removing them from the body.

Stabilized Rice Bran
Outer layer of rice delivers the most potent phytonutrient blend known with over 60 antioxidants, many of which are newly discovered vitamin E isomers.

Fructo-oligosaccharides
A probiotic; builds strong good bacteria in the colon.

Carrot Powder
A natural source of mixed carotenoids and other valuable phytonutrients. Excellent source of vitamin A.

Wheat Sprouts
Kernels of wheat which have been germinated. Sprouted wheat has more vitamins and enzymes than regular un-germinated grain kernels.

Beet Powder
Good for the liver and gall bladder because beets contain betaine, which stimulates the function of liver cells and protects the liver and bile ducts. Beets are a rich source of manganese, the trace element associated with the regulation of nervous system function. Rich in carotenoids such as lycopene and lutein.

Broccoli Powder Juice
Cruciferous vegetable associated with the reduced risk of cancer. Is a good source of iron and folic acid. Has potent antioxidant activity.

Soy Sprout
Soy is rich in isoflavones, compounds associated with decreased incidences of breast cancer. Soy also contains a newly discovered element called genistein, which is known to help block the nutrient supply to a tumor.

Millet Sprout
A grain that is rich in vitamin E, zinc, calcium, and magnesium. Is valued for promoting strength and energy. Millet contains the highest calcium content of all grains, has less phytates than other grains, is rich in B vitamins and iron, and is very alkaline.

Amaranth Sprout
A large leafy green plant that is an excellent source of protein, vitamins and minerals. One of the few broad-leaf plants that produce an edible and nutritious grain. Amaranth seeds are a rich source of squalene. Squalene performs as a strong antioxidant, being able to reduce or remove harmful effects of pollution in the body caused by toxic substances from the environment, including car exhaust fumes and industrial wastes. Squalene has been shown to benefit those who suffer from chronic fatigue.

Quinoa Sprout
One of the world's most perfect foods, quinoa has been consumed for thousands of years in South America. This is the only sprout that contains every single amino-acid. It is very high in protein.

Fruit Concentrates
Contains a rich blend of bioflavonoids, which make vitamin C work better and have been shown to protect capillaries from breakage.

Curcumin
The most potent component in turmeric, an herb that is widely used in traditional Chinese and Ayurvedic Herbology. Curcumin is known for its antitumor, antioxidant, anti-amyloid and anti-inflammatory properties.

Bilberry Extract
Enhances night vision and visual acuity. Known for its anti-inflammatory and antioxidant properties. The key compounds in bilberry fruit are called anthocyanidins. These compounds help build strong capillaries and improve circulation to all areas of the body. Bilberry fruit contains high concentrations of tannins, substances that act as both astringents and as anti-inflammatories.

Grape Seed Extract
A natural plant bioflavonoid extracted from the seeds of grapes that has a concentrated source of oligomeric proanthocyanidins (OPC) and is 50 times more potent than vitamin C and 20 times more potent than vitamin E. These antioxidants help to protect cells from free radical damage and also promote healthy circulation. In addition, Grape Seed Extract is rich in polyphenols, a compound that is high in antioxidants.

Betatene (mixed carotenoids)
Powerful antioxidant. Betatene is a form of natural, mixed carotenoids from Dunaliella salina algae. Carotenoids are antioxidants that help protect the body from free radical damage.

Lutein
One of the common carotenoids found in plant foods, lutein provides nutritional support to our eyes and skin. Lutein is an

antioxidant that appears to quench or reduce harmful free radicals in various parts of the body. Lutein has been linked to promoting healthy eyes through reducing the risk of macular degeneration.

Zeaxanthin
Zeaxanthin is a carotenoid found in many vegetables and fruits, particularly green leafy vegetables such as kale and spinach. It is one of the two carotenoids contained within the retina, and is rich in vitamin A. Promotes macular health and protects the cortex of the lens from free radicals.

Lycopene (from tomato)
Lycopene is a bright red carotenoid pigment, a phytochemical found in tomatoes and other red fruits. Lycopene is the most common carotenoid in the human body and is one of the most potent carotenoid antioxidants. It may help prevent prostate cancer and some other forms of cancer, heart disease, and other serious diseases.

Astragalus
A popular immune system enhancing tonic herb originally used in Chinese medicine for night sweats, deficiency of vital energy, and diarrhea. May help to improve blood circulation and strengthen the human immune system. Astragalus is used to prevent colds and flu, as an anti-viral and to aid in cardiovascular disease.

Milk Thistle
Milk thistle is believed to have protective effects on the liver and improve its function. It is typically used to treat liver cirrhosis, chronic hepatitis (liver inflammation), and gallbladder disorders.

Treatment claims also include lowering cholesterol levels, reducing insulin resistance in people with type 2 diabetes who also have cirrhosis and reducing the growth of cancer cells in breast, cervical, and prostate cancer.

American Ginseng

American Ginseng is used primarily for increased mental efficiency, stamina and for boosting the immune system and immune system responses. It is used to help relieve adverse effects of stress and fatigue. It has been considered especially helpful to the immune system in cases of fevers or infectious disease accompanied with a fever. It is also used in China to support the lungs and in the treatment of coughs and coughs accompanied with blood.

Gingko Biloba

Gingko Biloba improves blood flow to most tissues and organs; it protects against oxidative cell damage from free radicals (acts as an antioxidant); and it blocks many of the effects of PAF (platelet aggregation, blood clotting) that have been related to the development of a number of cardiovascular, renal, respiratory and CNS (Central Nervous System) disorders. Ginkgo can be used for intermittent claudication. It is mainly used as a memory enhancer and anti-vertigo agent.

Bromelain

A digestive enzyme from pineapple. Bromelain contains active substances that aid digestion and help reduce inflammation. Bromelain is useful in the treatment of a wide range of conditions, but it is particularly effective in relieving inflammation associated with infection and physical injuries.

Papain
Is a protein digesting enzyme from the papaya fruit. Papain helps break down protein to a digestible state.

Maitake Mushroom
The King of mushrooms – lowers blood pressure, inhibits the escalation of blood glucose levels, thus indicating anti-diabetic activity and stimulates the immune system. Assists in counter-acting chemo side effects. Maitake Mushroom may best be known for its cancer-fighting properties. It is also recommended for stomach ailments.

Reishi Mushroom
Reishi is an age-old medicine cited thousands of years ago in several texts and scripts as being a tonic for emperors. Regular consumption of Reishi can enhance our body's immune system and improve blood circulation, thus improving better health conditions. Generally, Reishi is recommended as an immune modulator and a general tonic. Reishi is also used to help treat anxiety, high blood pressure, hepatitis, bronchitis, insomnia, and asthma.

Shiitake Mushroom
Shiitake mushrooms contain an active compound called lentinan. Among lentinan's healing benefits is its ability to power up the immune system, strengthening its ability to fight infection and disease. A large number of animal studies conducted over the last ten years have shown that another active component in shiitake mushrooms called eritadenine lowers cholesterol levels. Shiitake mushrooms are known to stimulate the immune system by activating the T cells.

Amylase
Vegetable enzyme responsible for digesting starches. Added to support the breakdown of complex carbohydrates into smaller easier-to-absorb molecules.

Cellulase
Plant enzyme responsible for digesting the cellulose found in the outer cell wall of plants. This enzyme is not secreted by the human digestive system. Cellulase helps to release the nutrients that may be trapped in the cell wall.

Protease
Vegetable enzyme responsible for breaking down proteins, making them easier to absorb.

Lipase
Vegetable enzyme responsible for breaking down fats, making them easier to absorb.

In our fast paced world of eighteen-hour days and fast food, five or more servings of fruits and vegetables are an insurmountable task! Today many individuals often search for the perfect diet – one that will produce super health, strength, and resistance to disease. Unfortunately, there is not one perfect diet.

The best way to ensure your body is receiving the essential nutrients to prevent disease and strengthen the immune system is with an effective nutritional program.

Three scoops of *Ultimate Living's* **Green Miracle** can give you the peace of mind that you have given your body the nutrients it needs from all of those servings of fruits and vegetables that you missed. Every day I consume three to six scoops of **Green Miracle**. If you have never taken a green food supplement I recommend beginning with one scoop daily, adding another scoop per week until you take three scoops per day. Also, for those of us who travel frequently, capsules are available.

Ultimate Living's **Green Miracle** is truly a health food store in a can! This product is a pleasant tasting, nutrient dense mixture of live green foods. **Green Miracle** naturally contains essential vitamins, minerals, amino acids, essential fatty acids, lignans, fiber, and is a rich source of chlorophyll and enzymes.

Chapter Five

Natural Gifts: Aloe & Papaya

Often called *medicine plant* or *silent healer,* aloe vera has been used for centuries for its medicinal, health, beauty and skin care benefits. Most botanists agree, and historical evidence suggests, that the aloe vera plant originated in the warm, dry climates of Africa. However, because the plant is readily adaptable, and because man has been so eager to carry it with him from place to place, aloe vera now can be found in many warm lands. In the United States, it is grown commercially in the Rio Grande Valley of Texas, in California and Florida, and in specially-designed greenhouses in Oklahoma.

For centuries, aloe vera has been believed to be one of man's most complete nutritional substances. The most beneficial attribute of aloe vera is its ability to act as a biological vehicle for nutrients by increasing their efficiency. Studies have shown that aloe acquires its healing properties from its ability to heal from the inside out.

Aloe juice is an extract from the aloe vera leaf that contains over two hundred essential vitamins, minerals and amino acids. The aloe gel is the pulp of the leaves, a clear and tasteless jelly-like substance. This gel contains a "wound hormone" that accelerates the healing of injuries such as cuts and burns.

Lignin is found in the leaf gel. It is particularly noteworthy for its ability to penetrate tissue, and carries accompanying nutrients with it.

Saponins (glycosides) are the plants' active immune system. They have a cleansing and antiseptic capability. Containing powerful pain-killing properties and exhibiting certain abilities as antibacterial and virucidal agents, they can help humans fight fungal infections, combat viruses, and boost the effectiveness of certain vaccines. In addition, their natural tendency to ward off microbes may be especially useful for treating fungal and yeast infections.

Anthraquinones fight fungal infections, inflammation, bacteria, parasites and aid in metabolism, cellular respiration and growth. They inhibit formation of tumors by interfering with the growth of RAS cells, which are a precursor to certain types of cancer. It is believed that some anthraquinones cut off the blood supply to tumors, depriving them of their nutrients, thus slowing the growth.

The aloe plant may look like a cactus, however it is a member of the lily family. The leaves provide a natural source of many nutrients.

The remarkable health giving qualities of the aloe vera plant are due not only to the number of nutrients it contains, but also to the fact that the nutrients are in a natural balance.

Scientific researchers have determined aloe vera is an amazingly rich source of over two hundred naturally occurring nutritional substances that assist in building the immune system and maintaining good health.

Aloe has earned a reputation for providing the body with the necessary components to heal itself. Recent studies reveal aloe vera contributes four principle internal benefits:

 As an excellent delivery system of nutrients to the cellular level, aloe vera works as a carrier by helping the body better assimilate nutrients.

Aloe vera helps boost the immune system. Specialized aloe polysaccharide molecules help to open receptor sites into the bloodstream, which allow nutrients to reach the cells rapidly. Therefore, the cells responsible for reading viruses and setting the chain of events in motion to produce antibodies are strengthened. In chronic and degenerative diseases the immune system does not function correctly. Aloe vera has strong properties to build the immune system, and at the same time normalize and strengthen at the cellular level.

<u>Aloe vera aids in relief of gastrointestinal disorders.</u> Aloe vera helps to detoxify the bowel, neutralize stomach acidity, relieve constipation and restore gastrointestinal pH balance. The gastrointestinal tract is a key location for immune functions. There are concentrations of immune (i.e. lymphoid) tissue throughout the intestines.

 <u>Aloe vera helps relieve pain and inflammation.</u> Aloe vera contains anti-inflammatory fatty acids that inhibit the auto-immune reaction associated with certain forms of arthritis in which the body attacks its own tissues. Reducing inflammation reduces inflammatory damage. Aloe is an effective part of the healing process with regards to degenerative diseases as well as more common injuries such as cuts and burns.

Another important effect of aloe is the promotion of phagocytosis. This is the process by which the immune system mops up and eliminates bacteria and other infectious agents from the body. Aloe is a general stimulant and regulator of immune system action.

Improved phagocytosis is very important for the body's detoxification and cleansing mechanisms. It is believed the primary cause of chronic disease arises from the accumulation of toxins in the cells and tissues of the body. Aloe has been clearly shown to have bactericidal and fungicidal action, therefore, aiding the body in detoxification of harmful toxins.

Aloe vera activates scavenging macrophages and neutrophils in the immune system to enhance clean-up operations in the lymphatic system. Aloe assists in cellular growth and reproduction of cells with increased oxygen consumption.

Cells with increased oxygen levels have a higher energy supply. It is a matter of clinical observation that individuals with high-energy cellular activity are healthy, while individuals with unaccountable low cellular energy are more prone to fatigue, illness and disease.

For thousands of years aloe vera has been called *the silent healer.* *Ultimate Living* has combined the power-packed aloe vera whole-leaf juice and inner gel with organic papaya to formulate *Ultimate Living's* **Aloe-Papaya**. The combination of both juices is specifically processed to maximize the content of polysaccharides and other beneficial active ingredients.

Aloe-Papaya delivers much needed energy to the immune system to cleanse, detoxify, heal and repair.

Scientists have discovered papaya to have many healing and beneficial properties. This wholesome fruit contains many vital nutrients needed to maintain wellness. Recent nutritional studies found papaya to be packed with an abundance of enzymes, vitamins, minerals, and large quantities of carotene.

In fact, every part of the papaya tree is said to have some medicinal value. A substance found in papaya called *papain*, which is present in all parts of the tree and fruit, is an excellent aid to digestion, a powerful antioxidant, and it assists in maintaining energy levels.

Papaya also helps the body to produce more arginine. This is an essential amino acid that activates human growth hormones.

These hormones are important for cell rejuvenation and for rebuilding cells in the liver, muscles, and bones.

Papaya is a very alkaline fruit making it useful for soothing acid indigestion, heartburn and aiding in digestion. Enzymes found in papaya fruit help to digest proteins, fats, and starches. The digesting enzymes found in papaya assist the body's own enzymes in assimilating nutrients which are highly beneficial for energy and rejuvenation of healthy cells.

In addition, papaya is rich in vitamin C. Vitamin C has a positive affect on virtually every organ in the body and is required for life. The nature of our diets often leads to a lack of this essential nutrient. This deficiency may be a contributor to illness and chronic disease. Vitamin C plays a crucial role in building and maintaining our tissues and fortifying our immune systems.

Ultimate Living's Aloe-Papaya

Is an excellent carrier of nutrients to the cellular level

May stimulate immune response to fight cancer

Assists in regulating blood sugar

Helps to reduce pain & inflammation of arthritis

Acts as a detoxifier for intestines and organs

Aids in relief of gastrointestinal disorders

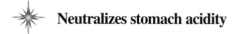 **Neutralizes stomach acidity**

AND...

Is delicious, powerful and the perfect pH balance with *Ultimate Living's* **Green Miracle powder!**

Chapter Six

Good Common Sense

The key to good health depends upon making good lifestyle and diet decisions. The state of your health today is a direct result of decisions made yesterday. Deficiencies in yesterday's diet can lead to weakness, fatigue, deterioration of healthy cells and most importantly, lead to a compromised immune system. Good health requires daily maintenance and care.

A diet rich in fresh vegetables and fruits is the foundation for wellness, but additional steps must be taken to build, strengthen, achieve and maintain optimum health. It is no secret that our food today is over-processed, over-cooked and low in vitamins due to nutrient deprived soil. To remedy this situation there are steps we can take which will ensure our body is receiving everything it needs to be its very best.

Key Steps to Optimum Health

 Eat 5 or more servings of vegetables and fruits daily (organic if possible)

 Add something "LIVE" to every meal (Green Miracle is Live!)

 Drink plenty of pure water

Exercise

Eliminate stress

Be sure to get enough sleep (6-8 hours per night)

Take quality nutritional supplements

Organic vegetables and fruits contain no harmful chemicals. This takes a lot of strain off of vital organs, such as the liver and kidneys, and in turn, saves valuable body energy. Fruits and vegetables are live foods. Organic foods contain higher amounts of minerals, vitamins and essential nutrients.

A **diet** must be well-balanced to include all food categories. No one food or food group should be eaten exclusively for the purpose of preventing a specific disease or for maintaining optimum health. Our body needs assistance from a variety of food sources that include minerals, vitamins, enzymes, protein, amino acids, antioxidants, calcium, fiber, etc. Important and essential nutrients can be found in all food groups.

Water: Drinking plenty of pure water is vital in keeping the body hydrated and flushed of harmful toxins. Remember, the easy way to calculate the ounces of water needed for your body to function properly is to take your weight and divide in half. The result equals the ounces of water your body requires, and should receive daily to function at its best.

Exercise: Set aside a time in your day to exercise. Exercise does not have to be complicated. It can include a simple walk around the block, lifting light weights at home, stretching, or taking the stairs instead of the elevator.

If an individual does not exercise to some degree daily, the lymphatic system becomes blocked and toxins remain in the body leading to illness and disease. Exercise is excellent for increasing oxygen circulation, strengthening heart muscles, lowering cholesterol, reducing high blood pressure, and improving glucose tolerance, which is poor in diabetics and often in heart disease patients.

Exercise promotes muscle and bone development, reduces stress, alleviates depression, and last but not least... helps us maintain a healthy weight.

Stress: Virtually everyone experiences stress to some degree. If you have a job, you know what stress is... If you have family, you know what stress is; and if you are single...you know what stress is.

The U.S. Public Health Survey estimates that seventy to eighty percent of individuals who visit a physician suffer from a stress-related disorder.

Stress is unavoidable in normal living. The most important aspect of stress is not the knowledge that we are under stress, but the way we handle it. Prolonged stress is harmful and can affect our health in many different ways. An estimated forty-five million individuals suffer from chronic or severe stress related headaches. Studies have shown many stress-related headaches can be relieved by simple-diet changes. Research scientists have found that when fried foods, dairy products, salt and acid-producing foods are eliminated, while dark green leafy vegetables and fruits are increased in the diets of headache sufferers, most have less episodes of pain, and in some cases complete elimination of headaches.

Sleep: Sleep is another necessity for obtaining and maintaining wellness. It is an essential part of daily life and determines our state of health. Sleep is a restorative process that replenishes nerve energy needed for many body processes. Lack of sleep can tax the heart and lead to many diseases such as chronic fatigue syndrome, high blood pressure, fibromyalgia, depression, and may impair immune function.

Nutritional Supplements: It is most important that we supplement our diets with high-quality nutritional supplements. The immune system can only fight disease when it is functioning properly. In order to function properly, our bodies have to take in proper nutrients to build and strengthen cellular structure.

According to Congress, Public Law 103-417, 103rd Congress, 1994: Scientific studies proved, "There is a link between ingestion of nutrients or dietary supplements and the prevention of chronic diseases such as cancer, heart disease and osteoporosis, and clinical research has shown that several chronic diseases can be prevented simply with a healthful diet, such as a diet that is low in fat, saturated fat, cholesterol, and sodium, with a high proportion of plant based foods."

Pets need veggies too! Our pets are suffering from many of the same diseases and disorders that we, as humans, confront. Our animal friends are usually fed diets of processed food (sound familiar?).

Just like humans, they are exposed to toxins in their water and the environment. Look at the epidemic of skin problems, allergies, and autoimmune disorders like lupus and cancer even in young animals.

Our pets' immune systems are being taxed by the same dietary and environmental stresses that affect our health. We need to see that their immune systems have the ammunition to fight for optimal well-being.

We have all heard people say, "dogs are carnivores, and carnivores are meat eaters." However, scientific studies have shown that diets in which animals are fed meat alone generally have unhealthy coats, teeth and bones. This is due to a lack of adequate vitamins and minerals and the fact that meat is deficient in calcium.

The natural diet for wild dogs and cats is varied. They eat not only the meat of their prey, but also the bones, the organs, and the intestines that often contain assorted vegetable matter consumed by the prey. Domesticated animals have diets that barely resemble their diets in the wild.

Ultimate Living's **Green Miracle for Pets** is super nutrition for our four-legged friends that offers many of the nutrients found in nature. With a superior selection of phytonutrients, **Green Miracle for Pets** also contains high quality protein, essential fatty acids and immune boosting herbs.

Green Miracle for Pets great tasting (pet's love them!) chewable tablets are rich in glucosamine sulfate for joint support and arthritis relief, and contain strong bioflavonoids to help build connective tissue and improve the skin and coat. Your pet's circulation, heart, blood, muscles, liver and eyes can all benefit from **Green Miracle for Pets**.

Our pets give us so much pleasure. In fact, there have been medical studies showing that relationships with pets can speed healing, lower blood pressure, reduce stress...we may even live a little longer thanks to our loving animals! It is up to us to see that they receive the best care and nutrition possible. **Green Miracle for Pets** is one way to enhance and hopefully extend their lives.

Understanding the role nutrients play in all areas of health enables us to appreciate their value. Illness does not occur without cause. It occurs when we have compromised our immune system.

Good health is attainable if you practice a healthy lifestyle and take quality nutritional supplements.

Chapter Seven

Taking Advantage of a Miracle

Without a road map, we will not reach our destination of optimum health. It's incredible how many of us just jump into our lives and truck on down the freeway. We too often race our motors, and too seldom stop for any reason except to refuel. I had plenty of time to think about these things while I recuperated from cancer surgery. That's when I began planning my new regimen and putting it into action. Where YOU are is where YOU begin.

First, a little motivation. Every woman knows when she looks great. Knowing we look our best makes us stand a little taller and put some extra pizzazz into our walk, talk and facial expressions. We feel good. We laugh. We sparkle.

I have seen many lives going the wrong way on a one-way Health Street, turn around and head toward Miracle Street. My own regimen began with my fears. I *feared* another bout of cancer. I *feared* and believed my immune system must be inadequate. I *feared* sickness and death. But those fears motivated me to develop a maximum anticancer defense system for myself.

My new regimen included not only my new health maintenance habits, but also new spiritual and emotional disciplines as well. For example, when I see a lump, bump or bruise on my body and fear rises up in me, I have learned to face it with fact and with faith. The good result is that I take myself to the doctor immediately, learn the facts and ease my mind.

Beyond that, I *choose* to face each episode with faith, not terror. Since I still have fibrocystic disease in my body, these episodes occur periodically. I have had to change my attitude toward cancer from one of fear, to that of overwhelming confidence in God, my doctors and myself.

What I urge all of you to do is to build up your defenses in every way. I want you to get your hopes up and keep them up. Then I want each of you to make a no-nonsense commitment to making your lives and health profiles abundant and exceptional.

Here's how I do it.

Dee's Regimen

5:30 a.m. Rise and shine. Drink one 8-oz. glass of pure water.

5:45 a.m. 2 oz. Of *Ultimate Living's* **Immune Support Formula** and stretching exercise.

6-6:30 a.m. Walk for two miles around the neighborhood, enjoying the weather, fresh air and flowers on clear days – treadmill in bad weather.

6:45 a.m. This is our daily Bible reading and prayer time for Glenn and me – even if one of us is out of town. We start our day together.

7:30 a.m. First I take 1 *Ultimate Living* **Complete Enzyme** Time for my morning drink, which includes:

- 3 scoops *Ultimate Living* **Green Miracle**

- 2 ounces *Ultimate Living* **Aloe-Papaya**

- 1 Tbsp. Omega oils

- 2 Tbsp. Fresh-ground flaxseed

- $1/2$ teaspoon *Ultimate Living* *Ionic Trace Minerals*

- $1/2$ ripe organic banana

- a few organic blueberries

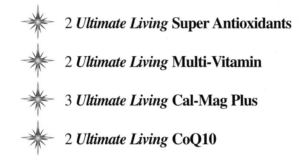

a small amount of pure water for desired thickness I put these into a blender and whirl into a delicious drink. I also take these vitamins:

2 *Ultimate Living* **Super Antioxidants**

2 *Ultimate Living* **Multi-Vitamin**

3 *Ultimate Living* **Cal-Mag Plus**

2 *Ultimate Living* **CoQ10**

Ultimate Living's **Green Miracle** is so packed with nutrients, plant foods, chlorophyll, vitamins, antioxidant factors, dietary fiber, vegetables rich in phytonutrients, herbal extracts and enzymes for digestion that there is nothing quite like it. **Green Miracle** contains numerous whole foods.

This green food actually represents a new generation of optimum nutrition. It curbs the appetite and improves elimination. **Green Miracle** contains no dairy, yeast or animal ingredients. It is suitable for vegetarians. I call it life's blood transfusion, or a "health-food store in a can."

All that potent nutrition, exercise and spiritual nourishment sure starts the day off right!

Take time for doing things for God, your family and yourself, and you can handle whatever the day may hold. Incidentally, my morning's nutrition intake more than supplies my immune system's maximum needs...but I don't stop there.

9:00 a.m.   I arrive at my office, well-prepared for the day ahead. I always have a twelve-ounce glass of pure water on my desk. Remember, the regimen I'm describing has enabled me to maintain the energy and stamina it takes to manage, develop and grow a company, juggle a heavy travel schedule...make regular radio and television appearances...fill platform speaking dates...minister to and encourage hundreds, even thousands, of cancer patients.

Some days are unbelievably hectic, but all that nutrition keeps me from sagging. For a midmorning snack I might eat a piece of fruit or a handful of nuts.

1:00 p.m.   I take 1 *Ultimate Living* **Complete Enzyme**. Lunch always features a salad or steamed veggies. If you do a lot of restaurant dining, these are always available. I use mostly olive oil and herbs for seasoning, and try to stick with the basics when it comes to salad dressings. After lunch I have two more *Ultimate Living* **Multi-Vitamins** and two more *Ultimate Living* **Super-Antioxidants**, plus 2 *Ultimate Living* **CoQ10**.

3:00 p.m.   I mix four ounces of pure water with three scoops of **Green Miracle**, and I also enjoy a snack of sunflower seeds, almonds or organic dried apricots.

6:30 p.m.   I take 1 *Ultimate Living* **Complete Enzyme**. For dinner, I choose grilled fish or a small portion of organic meat with lots of fresh vegetables and a crisp salad on the side. Occasionally whole grain pasta is on the menu.

9:30 p.m.   I sip a cup of herbal tea.

10:00 p.m.   Bedtime. Just before retiring, I take three ***Ultimate Living* Cal-Mag Plus**.

Every day I drink at least one gallon of pure water. You need to consume half your body weight in water each day. (Divide your body weight in pounds by two to get the number of ounces of water required.) Four times each year I use ***Ultimate Living's* Fiber Cleanse** to clean the colon. I also use Fiber Cleanse when I feel it is necessary.

When I tell seminar attendees about my routine, questions and arguments fly thick and fast. "I don't have time." "I can't discipline myself." "Who can realistically spend that much time, money and effort on themselves?" Let's take these objections in order.

Taking sufficient time for daily exercise, scheduled prayer and Bible reading, and fortifying oneself with the right food and nutritional supplements is crucial to well-being. Women are the family's appointed caregivers. But, if we don't first care for ourselves – in fact, make self-care a priority – how can we adequately care for our family?

Many women seem unable to grasp that concept. They pour themselves out in service to everyone else but themselves, which at first seems noble and unselfish. At some point, however, life will ask them a pointed question: How long can you continue to pour from an empty bucket?

It is prudent, right, and very wise to take all the time you need to strengthen your body, mind and spirit. The investment in yourself will spill over and benefit every other person you love. And only when you love yourself fully can you fully love others.

"I can't discipline myself" usually means that we, with all good intentions, put everyone else's concerns ahead of our own, or simply have just taken too much on. That means that in all the flurry of activities, we don't manage to make time to work out our own best strategies. I first began thinking about my own disciplines at a time when all I had to do was lie in bed while healing from surgery, watching movies and sipping tea – the only idle period in my adult life.

Schedule time to plan your regimen. Take the next step, and write it down on paper. Notice that I set a definite time for each step of my personal plan. Once you commit your decisions to writing and set a timeline for each activity, the rest is easy.

Your plan won't fail – unless you fail to plan. Take the steps outlined above, and you will have no problem with self-discipline. You will be able to live up to the important promises you made to yourself.

The question of how we can "realistically" spend so much time, money and effort on ourselves refers directly to our level of self-worth. Do we believe we actually are worth that much time, money and effort? It's always revealing to consider that question, and the real answer may shock you: IT IS realistic to believe you deserve to be healthy; IT IS okay to bless yourself.

God created us, according to the Bible, only a little lower than the angels. He has paid the ultimate price for you and me and every other individual in the world. We need to value ourselves more and raise our mental price tags.

Do the math! Which costs more – the money and time you'll spend on superb nutrition, exercise, prayer and study, or the extravagant costs in time, pain and cash a deadly disease can require? The correct answer is: Maximizing your health by practicing preventive medicine is the best bargain around! It is easier and less expensive to prevent sickness than to cure an illness.

Remember, your current level of health is a perfect reflection of your genetics reacting to the way you live and take care of yourself. If you are not satisfied with the health you have created, no problem. Simply change the way you live – your lifestyle – and you will see an immediate change in your total health picture.

Chapter Eight

Putting It All Together

Today, you are going to pick up your sword and shield in the battle of disease, fatigue and aging. There is only one way to stay healthy and that is to keep your immune system in top shape. Your immune system is your defender, your knight in shining armor. It can literally be the difference between life and death, and it is surely the difference in feeling and looking younger. So without further ado, let's give your immune system all the weapons it needs to fight the environment, bad diet (occasionally, of course), stress (you're trying, right?) and disease (it's everywhere!).

A properly functioning immune system is essential for resisting illness, and as I have discussed, the health of your immune system is greatly impacted by dietary habits.

Hopefully, you have decided to drink more water, eat more veggies and fruits, consume fewer dairy products, exercise, eliminate salt whenever possible, get more sleep, and de-stress.

Whew! It's hard work...this health stuff, but the payoff is WONDERFUL! Now that you are reversing unhealthy eating habits, let's put some icing on the cake (so to speak).

Green Foods

With environmental hazards, chemicals, stress, improper diets, mineral and vitamin deficiencies, and bad habits... can anyone really improve their health?

Yes... YES you can! It starts with making a decision to change your lifestyle!

It is impossible to maintain optimal health without eating natural, nutritious foods.

Today, more than ever, physicians and scientists consider nutrition the most important aspect to achieving and maintaining good health! Fresh dark green leafy vegetables offer marvelous nutritional and health benefits because of all the phytochemicals and phytonutrients in whole foods, as well as enzymes essential to the absorption of nutrients.

Now I'm not talking about eating an occasional salad and an apple a day. That is not going to make the nutritional grade. But, if your goal is to revamp your entire life, change the way you do some things, and make some sacrifices in order to absolutely achieve optimal health, then today is your day.

We need to feed our body the fuel it needs to be healthy. Poor dietary habits consist of two separate problems:

 We overeat what <u>we shouldn't eat</u>...fats, oils, meats, processed foods, sugars and starches.

 We under-consume what <u>we should eat</u>...fresh, organically grown fruits, vegetables, whole grains, seeds, nuts, and fish. Once again, the small lifestyle changes can and will make the difference in our health.

Add a green food supplement to your diet today! Make sure the one you select consists of all organic green grasses, is pure without artificial coloring, flavoring or preservatives and is manufactured to USP pharmaceutical standards.

Ultimate Living's **Green Miracle** meets all those standards and is truly a "health food store in a can." It is a superior formulation with eighty ingredients including over 8,000 milligrams of organic and all-natural nutrition.

Ultimate Living **Aloe-Papaya**

Add aloe to your nutritional regimen. One of nature's miraculous healing substances is aloe vera. Aloe vera promotes absorption of valuable nutrients in the body. It is nature's natural rejuvenator!

Aloe vera is:

An excellent carrier of nutrients to the cellular level.

An immune system booster. Specialized "aloe molecules" help to open receptor sights or paths into the blood stream, which allows other nutrients to reach cells rapidly. These aloe molecules deliver a boost of needed energy to the entire process of producing anti-bodies, which subsequently fight infection.

A strong pain and inflammation inhibitor. Aloe contains anti-inflammatory fatty acids that inhibit the autoimmune reaction associated with certain forms of arthritis, in which the body attacks its own tissues.

Aloe is inexpensive and does a world of great things in your efforts to regain youthful vigor. *Ultimate Living's* **Aloe-Papaya** is delicious and takes the benefits of aloe and combines them with vitamin rich papaya. *Ultimate Living's* **Aloe-Papaya** helps to detoxify the body, neutralize stomach acidity, relieve constipation and restore gastrointestinal pH balance.

Multi-Vitamin

The foundation of any nutritional program is a good multiple vitamin. Look for a high quality multi-vitamin designed to meet the needs of children, active adults and seniors. When selecting a multi-vitamin for adults there are several things to consider:

Make sure nutrients in your multi-vitamin are bioavailable, contain enzymes for absoption, and are in capsule form. This will ensure maximum absorption of nutrients.

 Make sure the ingredients are pure with no fillers like sugar, preservatives, artificial colors or flavors.

Select a multi-vitamin with a minimum of 400 IU of natural vitamin E. All-natural vitamin E is identical in structure to the vitamin E your own body produces. This increases absorption, makes it more active, and allows nutrients to stay in your system longer.

Recent studies show that individuals who have a regular nutritional program tend to be healthier and are quicker to heal than those who do not. A multi-vitamin is one of the cornerstones of a daily health regimen. Add *Ultimate Living's* **Multi-Vitamin** to your nutritional regimen. It is a synergistic blend of over forty nutrients in the proper ratio for men and women.

If we adults find it difficult to eat our daily intake of fruits and vegetables…imagine our kids! They hurry off to school, run from one activity to the next, come home and do homework, go to bed and then start all over again. The last thing on their minds is eating right. Fast food and food on the run are the norm.

However, studies show that good nutrition makes for better students and higher achievers. Even more importantly, we now know that nutrition in childhood has a dramatic effect on future health.

Five or more servings of vegetables and fruits a day for kids on the go are nearly impossible. And, let's face it…how many kids look forward to a big steaming plate of spinach or broccoli? I would not disagree that the best way to obtain our vitamins and minerals is a complete, well-balanced diet, but in today's world, realistically, this is simply impossible!

As parents, we cannot govern our children's diets as we would like. But, we can augment their nutrition with a good, complete multi-vitamin.

Ultimate Living's **Multi-Vitamin 4 Kids with Green Miracle** is a rich source of vitamins, antioxidants, minerals, essential fatty acids, and green foods. Specifically formulated to strengthen and build a young immune system, two of these good tasting chewables per day should enhance nerve and muscle functions, and stimulate mental alertness and healthy brain functions.

Containing **Green Miracle**, *Ultimate Living's* **Multi-Vitamin 4 Kids** offers some of those missed servings of veggies and fruits so when there is simply no time to say, "Eat your vegetables," you can at least say, "Take your Green Miracle!"

Minerals

Minerals that once filled the soil are now missing from our foods because of poor, depletive farm practices and over-farming, so we need to supplement our minerals as well. *Ultimate Living's* **Ionic Trace Minerals** provide over fifty minerals in nature's perfect balance. They are designed to replace the trace minerals now missing from our diets. Ionic Trace Minerals are small enough in molecular structure to penetrate the cell wall, unlike colloidal minerals which are ground up rocks and may be toxic.

Organically grown foods and organically raised meats and poultry, even organic eggs, all contain much more "good stuff" than conventionally grown and raised foods. Organic farming is environmentally friendly and produces food that is better for you. Organic food tastes better and contains up to ninety percent more nutrients.

Plus, chemicals and pesticides bombard our immune systems and force them to work that much harder. While our immune systems are fighting on the chemical front, some of our body's boundaries are left undefended and that is when disease can set in.

We need to give our immune systems as much of a head start as we can. Diet, good supplementation and the healthiest possible lifestyle are the only ways to do it.

This does not mean you can never eat another donut or miss a day of walking, but I'll just bet that once you get in the habit of doing what's right for your body and you suddenly find yourself feeling better, stronger, and, yes, younger…those donuts and sedentary days will be less and less appealing.

I do not recommend that you choke down hundreds of pills a day to stay healthy, but by adding a few supplements to an improved diet, and particularly those that I have mentioned here, I think you will find amazing improvements in your energy levels, your mental attitude and your appearance.

And, most importantly, your immune system will be armed with what it needs to protect you from disease and to help you feel and look your best. Remember, tomorrow's health is built on what you do today.

Testimonies

"After taking **Green Miracle** I feel great, and for the first time have energy to exercise. It has helped me decrease my high cholesterol and even lose weight. I love this product!"
P.A. – Missouri

" I love to mix my **Green Miracle** with *Ultimate Living's* **Aloe-Papaya**! It tastes great and my energy level, blood work, and overall health have improved so much that the doctors are amazed!"
B. T. – Texas

"I was diagnosed as having Type II diabetes. After taking **Green Miracle** for three months, my blood sugar levels are lower and now instead of taking medication three times daily, my doctor has lowered the dose to once daily!"
F. H. – Oklahoma

"After suffering with chronic fatigue and fibromyalgia for years, my friend talked me into ordering **Green Miracle**. I've regained my strength, pain is gone and I have so much energy now!"
G. S. – Arkansas

"My oncologist said I could take **Green Miracle** during my cancer treatments. Throughout this past year, I have not missed a day of work from my treatments. My blood counts have always been above the minimum in order to receive treatments, and my oncologists have been truly amazed at my strength!"
K. A. - Oklahoma

"I became ill after my home was sprayed with pesticides. Within three months of taking the **Green Miracle** and **Ionic Trace Minerals**, I was off the pain medication, and feel great. I have been on the products for almost a year now, and I'm a changed woman!"
W. C. – New Jersey

"*Ultimate Living* nutritional products have helped to restore my body back to health. I no longer have migraine headaches, my thyroid has straightened out and excess weight is back off!"
L. W. – Oklahoma

"Since being on *Ultimate Living* products, I no longer suffer from pain, depression, and frustration. I feel better and have a new lease on life!"
D. R. – South Carolina

"What a relief to finally have a normal life again! I have more energy than I've experienced in a long time! *Ultimate Living* nutritional products have made me a happier, healthier person and my visits to my doctor are only for my yearly checkups!"
P. F. – Oklahoma

"I suffer with acid reflux, high blood pressure and chronic fatigue syndrome. After hearing about *Ultimate Living's* **Aloe-Papaya** and **Green Miracle** I decided to give them a try. It tastes great and after several weeks I feel better, my digestive problems are gone and I have more energy!"
R. D. – Alabama

"My son was diagnosed with ADD/ADHD and doctors wanted to put him on strong medications. My mother told me about

Ultimate Living's **Multi-Vitamin 4 Kids with Green Miracle**. After taking **Multi-Vitamin 4 Kids** he is now able to focus better in school, his attitude has improved and no medications!"
L. B. - California

"Several weeks ago I was introduced to **Green Miracle**... It is a MIRACLE! I have suffered with a skin allergy for years. The hives and itching at times were unbearable. After taking **Green Miracle** and **Aloe-Papaya** for four days, red whelps are fading and the itching is gone!"
T. D. – Mississippi

"Before taking **Green Miracle** my triglyceride reading was 579. It should be in a range of 35-135. I was a walking stroke waiting to happen. After being on the *Ultimate Living* nutritional program for 5 months, my triglyceride reading has dropped and is on the way to normal range!"
P. A. – Missouri

Questions & Answers

Who should take Green Miracle?

Anyone and everyone who wants to ensure they are getting the proper amount of green leafy vegetables and fruits in their diet.

What is in Green Miracle?

Green Miracle is a mixture of over eighty different ingredients, including the "super green" foods (all gluten-free), herbs, enzymes, vitamins, amino acids, antioxidants and many other nutrients.

How often should I take Green Miracle?

<u>Every day</u> to build, strengthen and support your immune system. Also, **Green Miracle** should give you extra energy and stamina.

Can I take too much Green Miracle?

Absolutely not! **Green Miracle** is an all-natural, whole food supplement.

I am allergic to wheat. Will I react to the wheat sprouts or grasses in Green Miracle?

Our wheat sprouts and grass powders are free of gluten, which is a common cause of wheat allergies.

Will Green Miracle interfere with medications?

Green Miracle is an all-natural whole food. **Green Miracle** should not interfere with any medication. However, we recommend checking with your physician before taking any nutritional supplements.

Can children take Green Miracle?

Yes! We recommend children under 12 take *Ultimate Living* **Multi-Vitamin 4 Kids** with **Green Miracle**. Children love this delicious chewable tablet and it's an easy way to help your child receive the nutrients required to build strong healthy bodies.

Is there a difference between Green Miracle Powder and Green Miracle Capsules?

NO! Formulas for both powder and capsules are the same. Three scoops of powder and twelve capsules contain over 8,000 milligrams of all-natural nutrients! We recommend the powder for faster absorption and assimilation. Capsules are great and convenient for traveling.

If I take Green Miracle do I still need a Multi-Vitamin?

Yes! Your multi-vitamin is your foundation to build on. **Green Miracle** is a whole food supplement to ensure you are receiving your daily requirements of plant-based phytonutrients, and your nine servings of fruits and vegetables. Adding **Green Miracle** to your daily nutritional program will build your immune system and enhance your cells ability to fight off disease.

Is Green Miracle different from other green food supplements?

Absolutely! **Green Miracle** is comprised of grasses that are organically grown in our ancient volcanic farmland. Plants are processed and harvested specifically to preserve all enzymes, proteins, vitamins and mineral-rich qualities. It is a LIVE FOOD! Plus, **Green Miracle** contains over eighty different ingredients without fillers, preservatives, chemicals or dyes.

Closing

Letter From Dee

In 1987 I was diagnosed with breast cancer. My treatment and subsequent recovery began a journey that has become my life's work. Originally my quest was for information to help understand why I had cancer and to prevent its recurrence. I have been privileged to meet some of the world's foremost authorities on nutrition and cancer.

While all have many varying theories on the reasons people contract cancer and that some survive while others do not, most agree on one thing…nutrition is a major factor!

We sometimes forget that our bodies are a glorious gift, but let me tell you, when you hear the word "cancer" you are thankful for every healthy day, and are ready and willing to do whatever is required to maintain good health.

A strong immune system prevents us from contracting disease, and an immune system is best bolstered through good nutrition and a healthy lifestyle.

Are you starving for nutrition? You may be without even knowing it! A good diet promotes good health and prevents the onset of disease. Unfortunately, most individuals do not have a good diet, and therefore are very likely to be deficient in nutrition that is essential for their health.

The commercial food industry supplies a vast amount of colorfully packaged foods that produce calories and energy but contain no nutrition. So-called food without nutrition is dead food and is no better than starvation. We call it full belly starvation.

The simple answer to the lack of nutrition in today's world is supplementation with whole food complexes, which contain live food for live people.

There is no question in my mind that nutrition plays a major role in our health. Whole food complexes are the answer to widespread malnutrition as tens-of-thousands have discovered.

Green foods offer marvelous nutritional and healthy benefits including the ability to detoxify the body and fight free radicals. We should stick to organic foods in nature given to us by God. As much as is possible we should eat fresh natural fruits and vegetables. A good proportion of these should be uncooked.

And to make up for the loss of vitamins and minerals in what processed food we do eat, it is desirable to supplement our diet with a quality green food supplement.

Most nutritional companies dry plants at a blistering one hundred fifteen degrees. This kills all live nutrients and enzymes. *Ultimate Living* **Green Miracle** plants are dried at lower temperatures to ensure live properties are not destroyed. This rich super green food complex is one hundred percent <u>NATURAL</u>.

Green Miracle nourishes your body with phytonutrients, antioxidants, vitamins, enzymes, essential amino acids and many other nutrients to give you energy, healthy cell turnover, and to support your entire immune and digestive systems.

Aloe vera is another excellent source of over two hundred nutrients that deliver needed energy to the entire cellular system. Aloe vera also aids in detoxification.

The most potent nutrients are useless unless they can be delivered in an effective manner.

Ultimate Living has combined the power-packed aloe vera whole leaf juice and inner gel, along with the organic papaya to formulate **Aloe-Papaya** drink. This specifically designed formulation delivers the essential nutrients efficiently and effectively to every cell.

Having been blessed with a complete recovery from cancer, my focus has become directed to helping others avoid the awful experience of a cancer or degenerative disease diagnosis.

I am a true believer in the power of nutrition. Taking high-potency pharmaceutical-grade supplements is the best way to make a difference in your health, and selecting the right nutritional program is even more critical.

We can live better as healthy, vibrant individuals by combining a healthy lifestyle, proper rest, exercise, routine check-ups and taking quality nutritional supplements. By making these changes, one may add years to their life and life to their years!

Stay healthy!

Products

Ultimate Living's Products

Green Miracle Powder
Item #2010

Green Miracle Capsules
Item #2009

Green Miracle for Pets
Item #2006

www.ultimateliving.com

Ultimate Living's Products

Aloe-Papaya
Item #2028

Ionic Trace Minerals
Item #2016

Multi-Vitamin
Item #2011

Multi-Vitamin 4 Kids
with Green Miracle
Item #2008

1-800-360-0988

Ultimate Living!
by Dee Simmons

How to triumph over cancer and reclaim your life!

Ultimate Living is a positive story offering hope and encouragement to those experiencing a health crisis. It delivers the message that you must take charge of your life. Dee Simmons shares her journey from victim to victor and gives her daily nutritional regime so you too can find a new dimension of heath and helping.

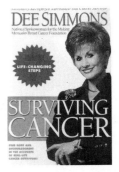

Surviving Cancer
by Dee Simmons

7 life-changing steps

Surviving Cancer gives direction to cancer patients and their loved ones who are desperately seeking help in the face of a shocking diagnosis. This book offers a sensible plan to set every cancer patient on a path to recovery. Dee teaches cancer victims how to take charge and apply her seven most powerful survival principles. Surviving Cancer foreword was written by Dr.. John Mendelsohn, President of The University of Texas-M.D. Anderson Cancer Center.

7 Days to Feeling Better and Looking Younger
by Dee Simmons

One of the biggest factors in looking younger is feeling your very best. Dee tells you her techniques for staying fit and youthful (and looking great) in her latest book, <u>*Dee Simmons' 7 Days to Feeling Better and Looking Younger*</u>. In just seven days, Dee and her book can put you on the path to a new, improved you ... feelling better and looking younger!

<u>Our Newest Publication!</u>

Natural Guide for Healthy Living
by Dee & D'Andra Simmons

Our greatest hope is that you will use the information contained in the pages of this reference book to guide you and your loved-ones towards healthy living – naturally!

For more information contact ***Ultimate Living***'s
Order Department - 1-800-360-0988
E-mail - info@ultimateliving.com

Website - www.deesimmons.com
or
Website - www.ultimateliving.com

Ultimate Lving, Green Miracle, and Dee Simmons are registered trademarks